The Failure of Certain Charms

Gordon Henry is an enrolled member of the White Earth Chippewa Tribe of Minnesota. His first novel *The Light People* won an American Book Award and his work has appeared in numerous journals and anthologies throughout the US and Europe. He is an Associate Professor in the Department of English at Michigan State University.

Earthworks Series
Series Editor: Janet McAdams

KIMBERLY BLAESER: *Apprenticed to Justice*
QWO-LI DRISKILL: *Walking with Ghosts*
HEID E. ERDRICH: *The Mother's Tongue*
DIANE GLANCY: *Rooms: New and Selected Poems*
ALLISON ADELLE HEDGE COKE: *Blood Run*
ALLISON ADELLE HEDGE COKE (ed): *Effigies*
GORDON D. HENRY: *The Failure of Certain Charms and Other Disparate Signs of Life*
LEANNE HOWE: *Evidence of Red: Poems and Prose*
DEBORAH A. MIRANDA: *The Zen of La Llorona*
PHILLIP CARROLL MORGAN: *The Fork-in-the-Road Indian Poetry Store*
PHILIP RED EAGLE: *Red Earth: A Vietnam Warrior's Journey*
CARTER REVARD: *How the Songs Come Down: New and Selected Poems*
CAT RUIZ: *Stirring Up the Water*
RALPH SALISBURY: *Blind Pumper at the Well*
CHERYL SAVAGEAU: *Mother/Land*
JAMES THOMAS STEVENS: *A Bridge Dead in the Water*
GERALD VIZENOR: *Almost Ashore*

The Failure of Certain Charms

And Other Disparate Signs of Life

GORDON HENRY, JR.

CAMBRIDGE

PUBLISHED BY SALT PUBLISHING
PO Box 937, Great Wilbraham. Cambridge CB21 5JX United Kingdom

All rights reserved

© Gordon Henry, Jr., 2007

The right of Gordon Henry, Jr. to be identified as the
author of this work has been asserted by him in accordance
with Section 77 of the Copyright, Designs and Patents Act 1988.

This book is in copyright. Subject to statutory exception
and to provisions of relevant collective licensing agreements,
no reproduction of any part may take place without the written
permission of Salt Publishing.

First published 2007

Printed and bound in the United States of America by Lightning Source Inc.

Typeset in Swift 9.5/13

*This book is sold subject to the conditions that it shall not,
by way of trade or otherwise, be lent, re-sold, hired out,
or otherwise circulated without the publisher's prior consent
in any form of binding or cover other than that in which
it is published and without a similar condition including this
condition being imposed on the subsequent purchaser.*

ISBN 978 1 84471 326 4 paperback

Salt Publishing Ltd gratefully acknowledges
the financial assistance of Arts Council England

1 3 5 7 9 8 6 4 2

Contents

Acknowledgements	vii
Beshig: The Failure of Certain Charms	1
Calendar of Wasted Seasons	3
Sleeping In Rain	4
Waking on a Greyhound Going West	8
Outside White Earth	9
Shell Lake	10
White Earth August Again	11
Leaving Smoke's	12
At Once You Recall the Thunder Song	14
Beyond the Refuge	16
When Names Escaped Us	17
The Failure of Certain Charms	18
Neesh: How Soon the Story Goes	19
Calendar of a Wasted Life	21
Entries Into the Autobiographical I	22
The First Door: I as Not I	22
The Second Door: I as Traveler I	24
Third Door: I As Alter I—An Autobiographical Meta-Tale on Writing	32
Fourth Door: I As Still Open I, from Spain	40
The Saxophonist's Meta-Americana Tour	41
October Naming	44
River People—The Lost Watch	47
Insulin Syringe Blues in the Key of Turtle Mountain	52
The Rumors Around Us	55
A Medicine Song	56
Jazz Tune for a Hiawatha Woman	57

October Minnehaha Avenue	61
Postmodern Rez Edge Inhalation: Paint Thinner Sublime	62
How Soon	63

Nissway: Directions from the Sovereign of Entelechy — 65

Calendar of Wasted Seasons	67
Gaween—Self Portrait:	68
Letter to the Agency Superintendent: November Becomes the Sky With Suppers for the Dead	70 72
Untitled Crow Abstract	74
Windows Against the Rain	75
Letter to the School Superintendent:	76
Primitive Epidermal Song	79
Imperial Lord Woosintoon	82
Abstract on Imperialist Cartographics	84
Song for the One Called Enemy	85
Lost Hunter—Under Hidden Constellations	87
Another Academic's Last Hope for Coyote Monologue	88
Simple Four Part Directions for Making Indian Lit	89
Hope Returns a Lost Whistle	93
If Only John Ashberry Were Gregory Corso, If Only Gregory Corso Was the Terra Cotta Horse on the Coffee Table With a Magazine Open to the You Can Be An Artist Ad	95
Directions to the Sovereign of Entelechy	98

Neewin: After Zahquod — 101

Calendar of Wasted Seasons	103
Ahwosso—Past	104
Song for a Sister Who Won't Let Go	109
Guessing at the Weight of Spirit	110

Profile of a Black River Member	111
Remembering Shadow:	
In the Art of Not Crying	112
Rez Edged Suicide Muse	114
Oshawanung Manido Equay	115
White Cloud Woman through a Southern Window	117
Sonny's Wake 2000	118
White Cloud Woman at Dawn	119
Dodem Dream Song	121
Recount to a Black River Elder	122
Pipestone: the Best Conversations that never took place	125
Before the Thirsty Dance	126
A Black River Elder Pretends	127
Traveling Among Strangers	128
Zahquod's Land	129
Blue Thunder Boy Healing Song	131

Acknowledgements

Some of these poems have appeared in other places; some will probably appear somewhere else—thanks to all those editors of journals and anthologies who were kind enough to publish some of these works.

Megwetch to:

all you thirsty dancers, to all the old men from Dunseith, to Jess
to Mary Anne, Kehli, CJ, Mira and Em
to White Cloud Woman, Bear, brother and sisters
Diane Wakoski
LaVonne, Silvia and Nieves
Robert the Photographer
Robert the Guitar Maker
Steve the Preacher Potter
G. Home
Terri and Larry
Nate (the Plain Brown Rapper)
my nearly adopted son Ray
Robert the Zimmerman
Tom Waits
John Prine
almost all of you magnificient Ojibwa writers and activists

In memory of

Francis, Louis, Zahquod, Wahsay Geeshig, Old Eagle Woman (or she who was also a Hunts the Thunder), Townes and Smoke

With hope for:

The younger people and
the generations on the way

Beshig: The Failure of Certain Charms

Calendar of Wasted Seasons

Moon of cats in heat
Moon of garbage dogs
Moon of the expired license
Moon of slick highway
Moon of telephone creditors
Moon of Anishinabeg names in the night
Moon of evaporated milk
Moon of uncles and Jack Daniels
Moon of woman against the lips

Sleeping In Rain

I

Wake Chants circle, overhead, like black crows watching her will stumble through weak moments. Like when she heard the carriage outside and went to the window with his name on her lips. Or when she looked over in the corner and saw him sleeping, with his mouth open, in the blue chair next to the woodstove. She saw them, dissembled reflections on the insides of her black glasses. Moments passed, etched like the lines of age in the deep brown skin of her face. She's somewhere past ninety now; bent over, hollow boned, eyes almost filled. She lives in a room. A taken care of world. Clean sheets, clean blankets, wall-to-wall carpeting, a nightstand and a roommate who, between good morning and good night, wanders away to card games in other rooms. Most of her day is spent in the chair, at the foot of the bed. Every now and then, she leaves and takes a walk down one of the many hallways of the complex. Every now and then, she goes to the window and looks out, as if something will be there.

II

Motion falls apart in silence, tumbling, as wind turns choreographed snow through tangents of streetlights. I am alone; to be picked up at the Saint Paul bus terminal. I fucked up. Dropped out. Good, it's not what I wanted. What is a quasar? The tissue of dreams. Fuck no, there are no secrets. There is nothing hard about astronomy, sociology, calculus or Minnesota winters. Those are just reasons I used to leave. To go where? To go watch my hands become shadows over assembly lines?

    A voice clicks on in the darkness. "We are now in Saint Paul and will be arriving at the Saint Paul terminal." Let me guess. In five minutes. "In ten minutes," the driver says. It figures.

III

My uncle's eyes have long since fallen from the grasp of stars. Now, they are like the backends of factories; vague indications of what goes on beneath the tracks of comb in his thick black hair. He was waiting when I arrived. Waiting, entranced in existence. A series of hypnotic silences, between words, that had to be spoken. Silences leading me to a beat-up car in a dark parking lot. I am too far away from him; too far away to be leaving for something further. I don't believe he doesn't like me. No, that's not quite what I'm getting at. It's something I saw when his shadow exploded into a face as he bent down over the steering wheel to light his cigarette.

IV

The cold white moon over houses too close together. Front windows, where shadows pass in front of blue lights of televisions. I am one of them now; a sound on wood stairs. There is a sanctuary of dreams waiting for my footsteps to fade.

V

The old woman dreams she is up north, on the reservation. It is autumn. Pine smoke hanging over the tops of houses, leaves sleepwalking in gray wind, skeletal trees, scratching ghost gray sky. She is in the old black shack. Stirring stew in the kitchen. The woodstove snaps in the next room. Out the window, he lifts the axe. He is young. She watches as it splits a log on the tree stump. He turns away and starts toward the house. He is old. He takes out his pipe and presses down tobacco. She goes to the door to meet him. She opens the door. She tries to touch him. He passes through her, like a cold shiver, and walks into the photograph on the wall.

VI

The mind bends over, in the light through a window, down and across the body of Jesus Christ as he stumbles through the sixth station of the cross. It comes to me sometimes, when I close my eyes. September sun in the old church. Smoke of sweetgrass in stained glass light. Red, blue and yellow light. Prisms of thought behind every eye. Chippewa prayers stumbling through my ears. Old Ojibway chants fading away in the walk to the cemetery. I look at the hole in the ground. I look at the casket beside it. I look at the hole. I look at the casket. At the hole, at the casket, at the hole, at the casket, at the hole.

The clock glows red across the room; a digital 2:37. My cousin lies in darkness. Another figure covered up in sleep.

VII

Dust swims in sunlight of an open door as dreams evaporate in the face of a clock.

VIII

"Get up, I said. It's raining and you, lying there. Get up, old man, I said." It is my uncle talking. He found the old man where he lay in the rain. He had fallen asleep and fallen down from his seat on an old bench I tried to set on fire when I was ten or eleven. The next week they buried him in the coolness of Autumn coming. Weeks after, the old woman thought she heard his carriage outside the window of her new room in the city.

IX

Cities of snow melt, blurred in liquid between wiper blades. We are waiting for the light to change. My uncle is driving. The old woman is waiting. Not really for us. Not for us, but waiting. I will see her this morning. This afternoon I will be gone. Another bus. Home. The light changes in the corner of my eye turning away.

X

The room never moves for her. It is not like snow falling, like leaves falling, like stones through water. It is a window, a bed and a chair.

XI

As the old woman touches me it is like air holding smoke. I am something else. Vestiges of prayer, gathered in a hollow church. Another kind of reflection. A reflection on the outsides of her black glasses. A reflection that cries when eyes leave it.

As the old woman touches me it is like air holding smoke. I am something else. Fleet anguish like flying shadows. A moment vanishing. A moment taken, as I am being.

As the old woman touches me it is like air holding smoke. It spins it. It grasps it. It shapes it in a wish. After that there is a mist too fine to see.

Waking on a Greyhound Going West

From far away
Rice Lake loons
call
the distance
darkening,
in whatever was
dream, fading
as crows
lift, piece
by piece,
from dead
on the side
of the road.

Outside White Earth

Vision and breath
travel away in
the smell of rain.
Next to a pickup
an old man stands
sleeping drunk,
hand on zipper.
    Leave him.
There is the liquor store.
Jukebox shadows of music
coming back around again
and again.
Torrents of faces
and women
shapes of smoke
opening mouths opening
restroom doors almost
as frequently.

At the touch of a hand
leaving, rain fills
your ears from the
roof, crumbling you
awake. You
stand.
    Hand on zipper.
Face against a phone
number
on the paint
of a peeling wall.

Shell Lake

There is
the penetration
of the smell
of Autumn wrestling
pine smoke
moving
into
startled
whisper
of wings
over water.

A formation
of geese
across the
lake,
in the
corner of
the eye gone.

White Earth August Again
for Bob Fairbanks

Your face travels
tamaracks rubbing
thunder clouds in red
Galaxy glass

To the funeral of
a Fine Day descendent

The last human shadow
from the cemetery
is the first to feast
The one who takes
the red hand of the mother
of the dead,
as she bends, stepping
into a black vehicle
where her tears roll
away in a cloud
glass face sobbing,
silenced by the
sound of engine.

Leaving Smoke's
To Gogisgi and Claudia

Black
wings sun glanced
green, crows
circle and half circle
snowfields before scattering
over old barns falling
slowly paintless
against the sky

across the road.

Your car shivers
to start, windshield
trembling, Sky, Blue
barked breath floating
white through
fences behind his
back and the door
opening she waves from.

At the stop sign,

the prism hanging
between door curtains
still turns
sun colors
on the kitchen
floor.

On M-66

something or the wind
moves outside
and turns his head to

windowed dusk's sun
leaving behind barns
with glazed empty
snowfield
beyond the prism
still.

At Once You Recall the Thunder Song

A village leaves every
door open
and no one returns

Old stone woman smudges
blue dishes under
the blue-scarred moon
at the guild hall

Bingo night eats up
the aspirin girl
on the blue television

Messages are never received
for one reason

For another a wild
dog upsets garbage

Auntie uses an air rifle
to silence the screaming
of passionate cats

None of the singers
will go into the mission

Under the influence
of gasoline fumes
a boy runs naked into
a barbed wire fence

The tribal custodian
dances with a BIA mop

The Chairman's deep in a dream
of information
about using information
more effectively

From steep bluffs
you look deep into
the river
held back by pointless dreams
and simple songs of home.

Beyond the Refuge

The road to Chi Mukwa's
runs guild hall backlit
as Jack Million's jiibai
stomps through
the Pine Point school

I've been trying to tell you
a diploma won't get you
the blonde with a pack of Kools
in the magazine Aunt T bought
with the hot dish ingredients
at the Red Owl
before you both
went out to shoot pool
at Icecrackin' Lodge
where medicine wheel
tattooed urbans
wasted a Stone boy
where we wasted ourselves
in Grain Belt, Pabst, in sentiments
only skins nearly numb
could live in long enough
to love.

When Names Escaped Us

The boy painted himself white and ran into the darkness.

We let the words "he may be dead, bury him,"
bury him.

We took his clothes to the rummage sale
in the basement of the mission
We put his photographs and drawings
in a birdcage and covered it with a starquilt.

For four nights voices carried clear to the river.

After winter so many storms moved in
strangers came among us
They danced
They shoveled in the shadows of trees

Then, somehow we all felt
all of us were of this one boy.

The Failure of Certain Charms

Dark flows from the memory
of crows, gasping away west
autumn violet at dusk.

Rock loves the Strawberry girl.
I hear his voice when he picks
her up on the two-track behind
the red house, so he knows my
dream of her fragrance
in the White Earth wind.

He also knows I carry too
many musical memories
to the gates of the graveyard
under the pines.

This is how it is with me.
I am behind Rock,
a distant flute among gestures
and shadows.

The Strawberry girl loves Rock
and night spins away
one song, one fragrance,
after another.

Neesh: How Soon the Story Goes

Calendar of a Wasted Life

Moon of dripping faucet
Moon of the cold school
Moon of the return of big geeshis
Moon of snow buried yard angels
Moon of accidental death
Moon of per capita fireworks
Moon of dismemberment
Moon of two holy clown piercings

Entries Into the Autobiographical I

"Live in the nowhere that you came from,
Even though you have an address here . . ."
—Jalal uddin Rumi

"Autobiography is the subject of personal logistics of knowable selves. How does one put I where one is or was? One needs a center, around which to build. The center is rarely an I."
— from the *Uncollected Writings of Dr. Gaween*

Evocation: From the wisdom of forebears to the clean clear northern streams, among Mississippi Band mothers and Otter Tail Pillager fathers, farther back beyond the current conventions of names and numbers, beyond the skins and skeins of dark heavy liquid, let me be in honor of those who came before, of the first bringer of light, of the charge of creation and the spark of Creator, let me live in a good way with the gifts of creation.

The First Door: I As Not I

I am not:
postmodern or modern; a sign, or a signifier, between signifieds; surreal or existential; neo-traditional or beat; transcendental or metaphysical; confessional, shaman, warrior, or sun priest; trickster, nationalist, exile or anthropocentric; psycho-dramatizer, or dishwasher safe, microwaveable, Sunday supplement collector plate; sell-out, or shade; or shadow chaser; or orphan boy, pop icon, trapper, trader, weaver, stone carver, powwow investor; or an angel looking backward; or an arboreal rodent, road kill, or coyote totem taster, clan speaker, band stander, or dream song; sonnet carrier, villanelle revivalist, or windigo washer; fumigator, suicide doctor, freeze dried mystic; or Lone Ranger lover, heaven seeker, or hell raiser; church leveler, drunken wonderer, sneaking, creeping, powwow playboy; or two thirds higher honor song singer; or hotel

lecturer, casino medicine keeper, or shell shooting, crow or
weasel; otter; or turtle, better or worse, water spirit, star gazing,
anthropological shape shifter; or check-out-line half breed hero,
or formula detective, divided between ordinary and
nonordinary; or authentic, natural, unnatural, deconstructive,
white hating, Eros, or ethos; or pathos; or apollonian, dionysian,
radical; or card-carrying, blood quantum physicist; or an apple,
golden, delicious, or rotten, or otherwise; or a tomahawk, hair
splitter, polemicist; or a two-stepper, ten steps from a twelve
stepper; or thunder being, or light being, writer of wrongs; or
pre-packaged, beadworking, pipe carrier; or pipe fitter,
ironworker; or artificer; of law and politics, of extraterrestrial
intelligence; or medicine wheeler spokesman, or blackjack
dealer; or chaos theorist, social contractor under federal control;
a plains clothes wardrobe keeper, sign wearer, or graffiti artist;
or epidermal epistemologist with nobody home, with an idea,
an ego, or a paper skin, or a well read skin, or next of skin,
intellectual, personal mythologizer disguised as a historian; or a
jessakeed, wabano, or a crystal gazer, or a new age bookseller
with a men's movement mind; or a biological timekeeper, a one
or only, to be forgotten , or a presence in absence, an absence in
presence, intense; or a psychic autobiographer, or an
archaeologist on the fringes; or a firekeeper/doorman; or a
burnout, exclusionist, a disallusionist; or a sounder of the
senses; or a sensual geographer; or a contradictor; or a great
waboose; like or as the king of ghosts; or a star lake ricer, an
either/or demanding neither; or a word waster, a word recycler;
or an apocalyptic, problematic poser, or a wholly imaginative,
word charger, gnostic; or a list maker, cataloger; or a
horoscopic, celestial reflector; or a sacred mechanic, in the
absence of culture; or a technological nightmare, flood
recollector; or a little person on familiar terms with cultural
giants; or a winter tongued salamander, licking the sky; or a
relativist; or a roadman, morning star man; or a hanger-around

the fort fetish hanger, with a broken chevy; or a first person, omniscient narrator of second or third confluences of consciousness; or a hyper-essentialist, parabolic, metaphrastic, nabi; or a Cherokee or a Sioux, Lakota or Dakota; or a house blesser, pre-packaged strawberry mist; or a car fragrance; or a savior; or a minority; or canon fodder; or a fry bread concessionaire; or an ethnic festivaler, wild ricer; or pinik naboop; or a fighting illini, an eagle or a hawk; or a peacemaker, a professor of any kind of highly classified studies; or a synecdoche, collective or unconscious, anima or inanimate; or an actor, or a plotter, didactic, or mimetic, or metahuman, onomatopoeia, or polytheist, or an agnostic; or a death song poet; or prophet; or a pilgrim; or a ghost supper waiting to happen, pure spirit; or nascent name on the material precipice; or a materialist with second-hand clothes, or a euro-muse looking for a place to land, or shall I claim more simply, I am not any of the above, on any line, on any form, to be signed below, or signified as other, with any other signifier between terms and conditions, esoteric to names, spiritual or otherwise, exoteric to names, European or otherwise, or shall I claim more simply: NO, I am none of these.

These are just some of my relatives. Some of them are buried between memories of turning leaves, some live as we speak; some of them are on the road; some have traveled many roads: some of them not good, some of them red, some of them not red, many of them red not good, many of them good not red, many of them both or neither. Still they are my relations and for them I am thankful.

The Second Door: I as Traveler I

I am a traveler:
outside White Earth, child
nearly dead from lack of air,
in the heavy embrace

of pneumonia,
in Philadelphia projects;

One who fears Superman,
One who fears Zorro,
a gunfighting son
of a Bear dodem father.

I am a traveler:
in the hands of sisters
in Catholic services,
in schools where the mist
takes the shapes of children
and eats lives whole and complete
in cursive and the arrangement of
letters.

I am a traveler:
one pitch from perfect
on a dirt diamond
in a bay area park,
where still train cars are
the main attraction;
in an Oceanside elementary
school where velocity
times memory is the
spelling game rocket
with your name on it;
in a classroom where
everyone wants to reach the flat moon
on the flat wall
from the flat earth.

I am a traveler:

like Anishinabe
grandfather Joe V.,
the dead pow-wow
dancer inside
the wooden box,
like all of us
who are outside
White Earth.

I am a traveler:
to the door of
Brunnette, the old Native man
at the wood pile, smoking
half and half,
the old Pine Point man
driving cousin and
double cousins to Shell
Lake,
the old Pillager companion
to the old woman Obahbaum
who sees father
in son, who hears
mother in daughter
who embraces
us and covers us with that
thick warmth of quilt
when we come in frozen
from nights of speaking
with sister speaking with
Norcross boys under stars.

I am a traveler again:
to that Pacific rock
where Zahquod hooks

up with Enterprise squadrons
and heads for the Gulf
of Tonkin,
where we go with Castro
from lessons on perspective
to shake mangoes down
from the tree of the grouchy
old Chammoran man,
where White Cloud Woman drives
us into the bush to find
bicycle thieves,
where the girls of the
island pay brother to
watch the corrugated metal
outhouse door
and kill shrews while they
piss,
where brother Bonehead beat
the hell out of two Cabreras
in boxing matches set up
by their father,
where brother Mukwa
found WWII shells in
Sumay caves.

I am a traveler:
to White Earth again,
briefly,
where to everyone's
amazement Brother K
drove one over the
left fielder's head
and silenced laughter
at Naytahwaush,

where after proving we could
memorize the apostle's creed
we fought with the heavy
sheriff's heavy son
at Pine Point during
recess from confirmation
practice,
where we found names
mossed over on brush covered
graves in the bush
near Rush Lake,
where we speared suckers,
trapped gophers, and sold the skins
to the old man
across from Grandma Marie's,
where we shot Uncle's pistols,
recoiled and raised dogs
under the dead
yellow Pontiac,
where the Loon mother put
out a chimney fire by herself
while we stood in pajamas
with Irene V. calling to no one
into nowhere
for help.

I am a traveler:
wandering in and out of
north suburban schools
we talked of organizing
an Indian student walkout
with Chickasaw Boston
and Skenadore, only to
realize we had the necessary

federal blood quantum,
but not the critical mass, so
we returned to geometry
and other subjects;
where Bury My Heart at Wounded Knee
was required reading for
smart kids,
where we continued
to wander in and out of
north suburban factories,
universities,
thunderbird drunk and in trouble;
where we guzzled and smoked
against the wall of the Teepee
liquor store;
where rats ate holes
in our bread and the Greek landlord
and his kids raised German Shepherds
to attack Blacks;
where we worked slowly
and stupidly toward a
first degree in the wrong lodge,
in the wrong field;
where we became
an expert on CETA
guidelines in two weeks
at the Big Fort job service;
where we made plans
on a park bench, near a Great
Lakes harbor, to leave
for Morroco with a beautiful
one-eared woman;
where we became expert
in time and materials

on the Commonwealth Edison site,
where we stopped the old carpenter
foreman, who went one too many
rounds with Joe Louis,
from going a round
with a local union man.

I am a traveler:
who married in a mill town along
the Rock River, not far from a stone
Blackhawk, carved into a cliff.

I am a traveler:
to Michigan to
a more advanced degree
in the wrong lodge;
where a shield teacher
came to us out of Ironwood,
where words and memory
saved Little Star from death
in Ann Arbor.

I am a traveler:
to Red River to
a more advanced degree
among Dakota and Turtle
Mountain people;
where Red Owl and his brother
took me to sweat;
where old man Four Star
and his son
took me to sweat;
where Eagleheart
and his brother

and Crossing Sky
opened their doors to me;
where we met Winona
at land recovery meeting,
where we drove into badlands
and told stories among
schoolchildren;
where we went to namings
again and again;
where Nagweyaab complicated her
own birth by reaching
out too soon;
where we learned of the thirsty
dance, where travelers gave us
thunder songs.

I am a traveler:
to Eagletown
where we sang with Two Crows
a couple of times, once
at the three kings feast;
where we tried to write
substance abuse reports
in the early morning, before
the BIA phone rang;
where we tried to work with
public schools for the Saginaw
Chippewa Tribe;
where we planted corn
and ran on the road
all summer in the humid
air;
where we fasted

and forgot about writing
novels, poems or essays.

I will be a traveler:
every year
from the year
Young Thunder Woman arrived
In Mecosta County to a year
in Spanish cities.

I will be a traveler:
to the thirsty dance lodge
where we lead scouts,
wrapped in willow,
to the ceremonial center
where we dance in place
where we look to the center,
the center we try to
remember, to heal those
others we love,
when the idea of self
becomes too much
for others
to carry, when we know
we are truly home.

Third Door: I As Alter I—An Autobiographical Meta-Tale on Writing

Not long ago White Crow stole my camera—an old Canon with a fixed, broken aperture. In the long run that was not so bad, but I could not present people with certain proofs, the proof people want from pictures without words. So I wrote words as if they were pictures in still lives like

> The moon stops the night
> traveling low in the tissue
> of clouds
> the glass is out of
> reach of the hand turning
> over.
> in the morning
> the head is framed by
> window by deep August
> light, crossing through the
> play of leaves.

Then—and this was before White Crow stole my camera—some woman in a graduate school fiction workshop said, "Why don't you write about Indians having their land stolen?" So I thought pictures aren't good enough; people not only want to see, they want to know something about the picture. "What does the one who makes the picture think of the picture?" I had to ask myself. Being of sound mind and limited vision, this presented problems for me, since it was after all difficult for me to see anything with clarity, whether it was part or whole, stationary or moving. So I tried again.

> Vision and breath
> travel away in the smell
> of rain.
> Next to a pick-up
> an old man stands
> sleeping drunk,
> leave him,
> there is the liquor
> store, jukebox shadows
> of music…

I tried to put myself in the picture, but I was unclear and still there was no stolen land in the poem. Then some road poet, bear writer—who I will call Spotted Eagle—told me "it's all metaphor." That was good because I was naïve enough to believe him and that was good because it made me forget the focus of the woman in the fiction workshop. So I turned my head again.

> Rice Lake loons call
> the distance darkening,
> in whatever was dream
> fading,
> as crows lift piece
> by piece from the dead
> on the side of the road.

When I showed my work to Spotted Eagle he said, "That's good, you've got crows and you've got road, keep putting those in and people will say they're metaphors." So I camped at windows, watching for crows, looking for metaphors. I saw sun flash in violet and green on the wings of one crow on top of Ramon's Mexican Restaurant, but I knew they'd nail me in writing workshop if I used the word "violet," so I refrained from opening any stanza with what I saw and I turned over poetic words in my mind. (I thought of a word I'd seen in a writing workshop, iridescent for the colored light on the wing, then I thought green? Cedar green? No, lighter and streaked with light and other colors.) By then I knew I was in trouble, and I was losing all interest in writing, when I met White Crow at a poetry reading. The reading itself was uneventful—four people read and five people listened. But after the reading White Crow said "Creeley," and Spotted Eagle, who read with us, said "Whitman." Thinking it was my turn I said, "Williams." They both turned, at the same time. "Yeah, Williams." I felt good and started humming "I Can't Help It If I'm Still In Love With You," while they went on: "Rexroth," White Crow said. "Neruda," Spotted Eagle replied. It went on like this for a long time, each poet talking about his influences, style, and appearances on the page. I listened for a while, until I grew sleepy. I drifted back to the car, hoping Spotted Eagle would follow soon, since we had to return from the university town we were in to the university town we came from. After a handrolled velvet smoke I fell asleep in the back of my blue nova.

I dreamed as I still do of my father's life. How he told me of the last time he saw his father.

I was in the back seat of the car. We were riding outside the reservation. My father told me to go to sleep. That was the last time I saw him.

Then I was with my father on the reservation, in the rooms where he slept, in the house of the old people, my great-grandparents. There was a past I couldn't live in, a past of languages and words I never learned, a past of words my father couldn't share. So as a child I was never a speaker and the comfort I received grew not out of words, but out of the resilience of a Native presence of my father's grandparents and their ways. They took him in and raised him when my father and his brother and his sisters had no one else. And I saw the face of the old ones then. When I stopped thinking of myself I knew who I was and where I came from, and I believed in this dream the way I believe that the spirits of the ones who raised my father raised me up. So I wrote

> Wake charms circle overhead, like black crows watching her will stumble through weak moments. Like when she heard the carriage outside and went to the window with his name on her lips. Or when she looked over in the corner and saw him sleeping, with his mouth open, in the blue chair, next to the wood stove. She saw them, dissembled reflections on the insides of her black glasses..

. The old woman dreams she is up north, on the reservation. It is autumn. Pine smoke hanging over the tops of houses, leaves sleepwalking in gray wind, skeletal trees scratching ghost gray sky... Out the window, he lifts the axe. (He is young.) She watches as it splits a log on the tree stump. He turns away and starts toward the house. (He is old.) He takes out his pipe and presses down tobacco. She goes to the door to meet him. She opens the door. She tries to touch him. He passes through her, like a cold shiver, and walks into a photograph...

(from Sleeping in Rain)

Then I was a boy again. Outside my maternal grandmother's house, at the place where we lived when we returned to White Earth. I stood in the grass, watching shadows grow long into the road. The old woman was watching me from a window, her head framed by the light in the kitchen. (She told me later she saw me talking to myself.) I was alone, wrapped up in a game I made up. In the game I took two small men, each made of molded plastic, and I put them in a box. I cut a hole in the box. I called it a door. Then I talked to myself and I sang to myself and I shook the box as I watched the shadows grow into the road. In time, one of the men would fly out the door of the box and the man who stayed inside, I called him the winner. In time I brought other men into the game and I gave some of the men names, sometimes the men in the box would fly out of the door simultaneously, so I would send them back to try again, until one or the other was left inside. I can't remember when I quit playing that game.

I told White Crow of my dream in the nova, but he wasn't interested. Then I showed him the words I wrote. "It's fiction," I said. "No," he said. "It's more like poetry. It's not realistic. There's too much 'I' and the prose is weak." (Later, most of the people in the fiction workshop agreed with him.) "Try this," he said, "after you write, put your papers on an ironing board and run them under an iron. Not a hot iron, but a warm iron. If you make the iron too hot some words will stick to the metal, but if the iron's too cool the words and paper won't get flat enough." Flat, I thought, seems right, and White Crow seems believable. "But," I said, "won't the words have a metallic trace to them?" White Crow blinked twice, once with light, once darkly. "Yes, but that's what you want, flat and a bit of iron, or aluminum." Also he said, "The iron brings out the material in the paper. The warmth of the metal helps the paper remember its life as a tree, as material. You follow?"

I don't remember going home after that. After a few more months, I got pneumonia for the second time in my life. My life turned then. I completed my master's degree and I went to Ann Arbor to start on another degree. But some element of my sickness held on. I had no desire to live or write. People entered my life and after speaking to an elder from Ironwood, I knew I had to get away. I had become part of other people's sickness as well; my first daughter, Kehli, almost choked to death while I partied with friends.

I tried then to leave Ann Arbor. When my wife and I were packing our things, White Crow knocked on the sliding glass doors. As I carried boxes out to the U-Haul, White Crow said, "Stop, I'll get a picture of you guys in front of the apartment." Then he picked up the Canon from the table and we stood there waiting. I remember thinking: it won't come out right; the light is no good and he doesn't know the camera. He took the picture. After a few minutes he left and we went back to packing.

My family and I went on to North Dakota. Later on, in the spring, when my wife and I wanted to take a picture of a double rainbow, we realized that we had no camera. It wasn't in the unpacked box marked miscellaneous and it wasn't in the closet, with the boxes of pictures. But North Dakota was good, with or without the camera. I gradually felt myself healing. I wrote nothing for years, until I gave in to giving up writing. This led me to

> How Soon
> The story goes from in a rainfall
> to sister walking a field
> browned autumn. And when she arrives
> winter has come, so the old man
> rises from his chair, picks up
> matches, pipe and tools, and
> walks out to begin again.
>
> The sculptures grow by the day,
> birds in ice, recognizable
> eagles, a bear who began
> as a man in a moment of dance
> He does this in ice, all
> winter carving at dusk.
>
> And sister after walking a field
> browned autumn arrives, watches
> from the east window, waits,
> goes out to him in spring,
> taps him on the shoulder,
> and points to the pools
> of water he's standing over.

I also met new teachers outside of the university. An elder named Francis Cree took the time to meet with me, whenever I went up to Turtle Mountain. From him I learned strength and acceptance. He brought me into ceremonies, he opened his ceremonies to me and taught me. At the same time I started working as a writer in the schools in North Dakota. I traveled all over the state, teaching poetry and telling stories, many of which were about creating stories. Through Francis, through storytelling, I grew to recognize the gifts of creation. I saw my wife and children anew. I began to understand the deep and profound ways of seeing that being in ceremony involved. Those ways of seeing and understanding helped me to recognize the stories in all things; these ways of seeing helped me to try and see the cumulative past in the being present. My life opened and kept opening. At one ceremony I was given a gift.

>The Story of a Blue Man
>As Strawberry (or He Who Walks Behind the Buffalo) prepares to cut me, Little Boy walks up and hangs the beaded man around my neck. After the ceremony, I receive instructions: feed him sweet things, put tobacco out, ask about him often. I do these things and I carry the man with me everywhere.
>Sometimes when I think I've lost him, he turns up inside a shirt I've left in front of the mirror. Once I found him hanging from a willow branch, after I spent a morning gathering wood. I've given him peaches and strawberries in summer. I've taken him to see moss covered stones and to the creek where my children play.
>When I think about him, I know that I am part of a larger family. I am part of Little Boy's family, Strawberry's family, Eagleheart's famly, White Earth families, Vizenor families and Henry families, the families of Belangers and Fairbanks, the families of Minogeeshik, and Oskinaway, the families of those who came before us in words and names, the families of those who will come after.

For years I never saw White Crow, though I thought I saw someone who looked like him at a conference in Wisconsin. He was sitting at a table with a couple of Oneida women. Live birds in cages were singing over their heads, so I couldn't make out their conversation. I almost went up to him—to ask about the old Canon—but a Cheyenne River poet going in another direction asked me to go to the casino with him, and I did.

I eventually left North Dakota and returned to Michigan. Since then I've worked for two tribes and two universities. Since then a third daughter has come among us. Since then I've given a beaded man to a Tuscarora elder. As for White Crow I've seen or heard nothing of him for a long time. I don't know that I'll ever see him again. If I do see him, I'll tell him to keep the camera. In some ways I believe the old Canon has always been his and he should keep it.

Fourth Door: I As Still Open I, from Spain

In the metro station at Moncloa, we pass immigrant African vendors. They sell Winstons and beaded jewelry. People walk quickly by us, sometimes nudging us wordlessly. As we ascend the steps into the sunlight, I am thinking of smoking, looking for the old man at the top of the steps. I know he'll be there at a card table, selling gum and lighters. I need a lighter. I approach him and ask for a lighter. He holds one up and grinds his thumb against the metal lighter wheel, igniting a spark. Then flame shoots up, straight, orange and yellow. At this moment I long for home, for the moments before the sweat fires at Turtle Mountain, where Francis and Louis tell stories, where Houle and Ecklebecker trade insults, where Old Eagle and I sit in silence on stones, listening, remembering, and looking forward to more stories.

"*Vale?*" the old man says, as the flame draws into disappearance. I take the lighter from him. "*Vale, gracias,*" I say. "*Megwetch,*" I whisper later as I take a smoke and think of many people, of many families, of home.

The Saxophonist's Meta-Americana Tour
For Joy H...

She traveled some roads
    layered with paved bone dust of
        haiku liars
She traveled some roads
    of spotted cattle remembrances
        smell and hillside grazing
She traveled some roads
    that ended in the closed eye
        of a sleeping giant behind barbed wire
She traveled some roads
    that opened to sleep and woke
        in cells breaking apart
She traveled some roads
    that were two roads
        both less traveled more or less
She traveled some roads
    beaded with blood
        smell of porcupine bygones
She traveled some roads
    that went up to doors
        with no knobs or handles
She traveled some roads that
    came out in back of
        the theatre where we shot at each other
She traveled some roads
    that moved like celluloid
        through synapses of light and dark
She traveled some roads
    with Smoke and Mirrors Woman
        no one would know the truth by
She traveled some roads
    with avatars of lipstick nights
        under a hoop of braided sweetgrass

She traveled some roads
        by star directions
                and satellite positioning systems
She traveled some roads
        completely naked except
                for earrings and jelly shoes
She traveled some roads to
        follow howls to follow moon
                and sirens deep in the interior of passes
She traveled roads
      that were all ears
             of corporate corn and sugar
                    beet hills
She traveled some roads
 behind combines of autumn,
      behind stone heated Mennonite
            carriages of winter
                  behind big Winnebago summer
                      retirement dreams,
                          behind young thunder storms
                              glassed in spring
She traveled some roads
        past giant fish restaurants with open mouthed entrances
            past a turtle made of wheels
                past statues of upright citizens
                    cast at the center of town

She traveled roads with no names
      singing the names
            of alcoholic beverages and
                  and automobile grillwork
                  and music as old as cuts and bruises

She traveled roads
    with baloney and cheese radicals
        with trailmix anarchists
            with sushi capitalists
                with fasters, who just finished a fast
She traveled under
    the influence of engine tumescence
        one eye on the radiator symbol
            one eye on phosphorescent road edge
She traveled roads
    that mushroomed into Shakespeare shapes

She traveled roads
    of puke drafts
        going to yeast
She traveled roads
    leading nowhere
        to where the middle
            always is
She traveled some roads
    to lose some behind
        never to find
  ahead

She traveled some roads
    exposing the hearts of still
        dying animals
            on their way to becoming road.

October Naming

Singers come out of the dark and wake me first. I know it is time to go, but Crossing Sky is slow and he already has a name. The old man said, "Come first thing..." in the morning, but Crossing Sky is slow and he makes me sit down to breakfast. He talks over coffee, toast and scrambled eggs. He talks slow and tells of the night the ceiling opened and someone told him about this medicine. He talks, says he is loved, that this is what we're doing, it's about love. I know the old man waits, the singers woke me, so the old man was already working. I was supposed to be there when the singers called. But Crossing Sky is slow. He rolls a red willow smoke and hands it to me. He rolls another and smokes.

Woodpecker darts through slats of light cut by trees. The fire has gone down, though stones still glow hot in the ash bed. A pitchfork lies in front of the fire. We knock on the old man's door. The old woman comes out. *You guys were supposed to be here early. He came out and started the fire. He went back to sleep when you didn't show.* She wakes the old man. I can feel his frustration with us. I should have left as soon as the singers came. We walk back out to the fire. I give the old man cloth and tobacco.

What color cloth should I bring? People stand in a circle around me. I don't know them. Some are old, some are shadows, some are whispering.

An old man steps forward he comes toward me opens his hands and gives me yellow cloth.

I reach for Mary in the dark. The baby is hot between us. She breaths through a stuffed nose and nudges her mother. Her eyes flutter. I kiss the back of her head and stretch to kiss Mary. On the other side of her Stella sleeps face up. I find my clothes on the back of the chair, where I read last night. I dress, make coffee, pour a cup and leave. I go north.

"Gete Kinew," he says as we come out of the lodge. I strain to break it down, syllable by syllable. I watch it roll from his mouth and I watch his lips. Behind him woodpecker hammers halfway up a young maple. I repeat it. Gete Kinew he says. Crossing Sky smiles, "aho" he says.

Inside we eat again, bacon, eggs, toast. Then Rose pours us cups of hot tea in metal cups. The old man rolls a cigarette out of a bag of golden Canadian tobacco and smokes it down to a pinch between his fingers. He tells a story about his father. *He had spiritual gifts. He could find lost things. He'd take a rattle. Darken the whole room and sing.* Then he tells me about names. I look at his eyes the light in their centers as he speaks. Across from him Rose weaves a strand of red willow through ash ribs of a basket at the table. The old man stands then walks into another room.

He comes back with a leather vest and hands it to me. Try it on he says.

I repeat the name all the way home. I try to remember the songs the old man gave me. I repeat the name as I drive 2 all the way to Grand Forks. I repeat the name and remember the songs.

Music comes faintly from the house as I approach the door. Stella is dancing when I come in. Mary is in the chair we found at the church sale. The baby is wrapped tight in a blanket, sleeping on the couch. I go over to her, whispering the name, singing as she sleeps.

River People—The Lost Watch

When we were river people
once in a while you talked different,
different because we were under
the influence of elders—their repetition,
a northern dialect of hands
coming apart in stories.

When we were river people
the sun made an alphabet
of light struck trees
while you sat on a stump
in the yard and rolled
tobacco from the plants
we grew
in the raised beds
by the power
pole.

When we were river people
the dog we took from dog death row
at the shelter got cancer and
we put her in the ground near
where young thunder woman
learned to hit golf balls
toward an old shirt on a stick
where every shot was lost.

When we were river people we made medicine
for Zahquod and fasted and sweat at dawn
for four days, following Eagleheart's instructions.
Zahquod drank the tea for a few months
and died the following fall.

When we were river people we put stones
in the mailbox to keep the weekend rowdies
from hitting it again while we slept
and we drove
to town every Thursday to
take Anungoonce to tap class.

There were boys after her after that
and we let one in.
There she held him close often and made sure
he got his needle before he stupored in
dropping sugar.

When we were river people
big leaf rhubarb grew,
wild turkeys walked in the mist
up the drive
a few big hens in front
and the gas man apologized when
he saw you talking with pwagun
early one Friday when you heard the news
about Zahqoud starting on interleukin 2.

When we were river people you listened
to Townes every day for a week of summer
'to live is to fly' he said 'both low and high'
he said with his cracked hard Oklahoma voice
he reminded you of Smoke
the week you watched his horse
and the belly laugh his goddaughter
Anungoonce let loose
outside the barbed wire
pasture fence as Seguili the horse ran.

When we were river people we lost power
for five days one winter, so we braced
ourselves on fallen logs when we shit outside
and we fed the woodstove and slept on the
floor and drove to Canadian Lakes to shower.

When we were river people
singing woke you one night
and you ran outside asking
the stars and the creator to help
you remember the words
remember the words
Gichi manidoo have pity
Gichi manidoo bring healing.

When we were river people Geeshik
Eway Abaat would not talk to you
though you kept asking to let your love
for her find its way to her, so you could
tell her about the shooting star and her birth
under a formation of white cranes
And so you could laugh with her
about when she was three,
when she came crying out
of the sweat with Grandma Rose.

When we were river people visitors
came with strangers and strangers came with
friends to bring wood and stones for namings
sweats and thirsty dance sings and all those
gifts Eagleheart shared with you
when you lived out west.

When we were river people deer
ran through morning by morning
one morning a string of them
one walking wounded outside
hobbling on three legs, an arrow
through the fourth, outside the
window as you made breakfast for all
the girls who came looking for Nawgwayawp
and stayed overnight after the dance.

When we were river people there was
no time for writing, too many people
were dying, too many children were
growing, there were too many ceremonies
to make, too much firewood to cut, too many calls,
too many fasts, too many trips to
White Earth and Turtle Mountain
too much burned gas
too many names requested
to be given, to people you know
who still don't know who they are,
too many appointments, disappointments,
too much tired talk, the difference between
going to sleep and staying up
already past deciding.

When we were river people
Crow knew just like you know now
a stone is no place for a watch
as you know what we call time
can't be made up with words
lost, or remembered, or held down

to earth, or be left behind
by blessings, forgotten, or be any more
than a relative of light, who returns home,
as bright clear sun reporting all
that has gone between rising and falling.

Insulin Syringe Blues
in the Key of Turtle Mountain

Who will take you
to the pink spirit house
in the Methodist sunrise cemetery
where the transvestite
sniffer inhales paint
on Saturdays
at the headstone
of some relative
five years gone?

Who will offer you
cash for crafts
Hunts the Cloud taught
you before you left
for Rocky Boy with Railroad
Martin the summer
your thirsty dance brother
came back from the war
without hands?

Who will keep the door
for the Sunday women's
lodge on those cold Dakota
mornings of reluctant
fires?

One windigo kahn
remains homeless, sleeping
in a vehicle with
a Lightning woman,
the other
sits in an elders' complex
trying to escape sitcom
evenings with a weak
bladder.

Still we got our ways of survival
our songs and our dreams
the lodges of our fathers
the hills of our mothers
we got our ways of survival.
I am in an IHS wheelchair
alone at home with an insulin syringe.

Who will light
our leader Pwaagun
when the council people
call for a blessing for
another BIA building?

Who will give you
the stories of Broken Arm,
the Light, Oshkinaway,
Many Eagle's Set
or your grandfather's
sunrise song, or his gifts
of finding lost people
while singing
in darkened rooms?

Who will
remind you of your
mother's last day
her refusal to eat
her helping you with
arbor flags as she sets out
the instructions for women
entering the arbor?

Who will name
your children?
Who will tell you
to feed visitors
the memegwasay
the people of the offering
plate, the strange seekings
of strangers?

One ceremonial priest
is out west working
40 hours a week,
another lives in Michigan
a professor far from his
reserve.

Still we got our ways of survival
Our songs and our dreams
The lodges of our fathers
The hills of our mothers
We got our ways of survival
I am in an IHS wheelchair
Alone at home with an insulin syringe.

The Rumors Around Us

Now
my skin brushes the last living flower of autumn
Blue and gray dogs circle the dinner of the least among them
I have talked to hot southern wind while walking away from home
voracious birds feed on the rotting flesh of an animal
struck by a blue nova, a few days past, into dry creek bed

Before the summer ceremony
one man tells me one boy standing against the enemy is
the real story of the dance you've given your life to
Another says it all comes from the thunders,
voracious birds wind through wires, land on and embrace
the transmissions of gossip, the questions of surveyors, the endless
appointments, the dates set, the machine receptors,
the persistent daylight hum of metal through copper, through
   silver alloys, their talons energized

In winter
when I am old I will go to a place where the climate
controls are few and conversations revolve around
body parts, lost organs of youth, the children out the window
washing the old convertible galaxy
voracious birds whistle in an ascent into wild cloud, as we'd like to
think there are faces there, of older ones, in the next storm coming,
in a rain called for by the spirit of a Sunday funeral

Now
your skin, my skin, the last meeting between us
seems all we come to hope for, in memory and touch
We find in each other a record, a few hundred songs,
spoken at those times when we gave ourselves up for
some other act of renewal, tied up in cloth, in prayer on some
faraway morning where we marvel, amazed at the turning, the ease,
the way voracious birds carry away the dead as if weightless.

A Medicine Song

A medicine song evaporates
from your sleep.

Dead yellow news
floats over the heads
of the homeless as
their hands come apart
in stories over a barrel
fire.

Jazz Tune for a Hiawatha Woman

                      You know where I'm coming
from:
On the same street past the tracks
            where last august
    we drained a few predawn
                quarts made promises against
    a mural of imperial oppression
on the wall of the workers
            of the world bookstore
                  (later closed up and reopened later
    as a Hollywood Video.)
                      Now
            a few tripped out
   two-spirit women skins
verbally fuck with
   a panhandling Devils Lake
         wino in a Viking shirt
                  outside the currency exchange.
As I make my way toward
            you over the bridge nicknamed
               "Two Suicides" (with a graffiti lightbulb
        launch point on the railing
and sprayed fluorescent sketches
              Of pornographic body parts, rubbing
      up against dollar signs

  on the concrete stanchions
                    underneath.)

            Try not to blame me that
   the pow wow windigo kahn got
               your cell number from

                              the table at the city park
          where I carved the digits
                    with a leatherman before I put
                              the last number down
     in blood I drew with
                    broken glass and mixed
          with a pinch of ash
                              from my menthol
     camel.
                    (He wrote it all backwards
     under his ANISHINABE name
                         on his fist)
          Just tell him when he calls
                         you love it when he calls.
                              He'll go back to dancing
               while reading the news in the
                         Circle just like he did
                    behind the middle-aged
                              jingle dress matrons,
               dangling their moccasin
                    matching bags with limp wrists,
     glaring under beady flora
               of woodland tiaras,
                         knowing and not liking
               the clown mocking their
                              steps behind them
          at the upper Midwest gathering.

          I heard from Spotted Eagle
                         at the halfway   house
               after he ticked off conditions for my
                         release from three freezing
     moons of treatment:

(No drugs No pot No speed No black cadillacs No more shooting your
grandfather's IHS painkiller prescriptions No drinking No driving No
parties No bad influences AA twice a week ay You go to meetings at our
Lady of Whatyacall or you can go Tuesdays at the Indian center just give
in to a higher power and keep up the sober interior monologues).

                  your Ma's still hanging on
to that Big Knife bricklayer
                  who ate the leftovers
    I brought from Hard Times Café
            for you
                the day I walked all the way
        back here
In clothes I found in a garbage
        bag in the back of a dodge
              pickup parked in the drive
    at Uncle Salem's
                only to find you'd gone north
        for a funeral.

Could it be more complicated?
        At 10 I tracked deer with my
            Aunt and waited by a tree
                in falling snow, shot
                    my last round into the air
            just to let her know
        where I was before it got
                  too late to search for me.

Nine years later, at the U
        I took classes, studied philosophy,
            European history and social
                linguistics, chemical tables
            world religions and I still managed
    to remember my name and

                        the names of relatives and places.

I've lived and traveled
                                with no destination to speak of.
                        I even stopped myself in the
                                    middle of dreams just to wake up
            So I would remember faces
                                    conversations, the speakers
        And the voices, the mists and animals
                            the roads and enclosures,
                the running, the flying and
                                the fear dreaming of immobility brings.

Still,
            as I make my way back
                        to you, stand before another door
                                    I know that inside there is
                No one, as your having left
                                remains the hand on another
door of my arrival.

October Minnehaha Avenue

On the red formica table
over Pontiac keys, a cup of coffee
and a twenty
for enough gas to get home
talk is nearing enough to fire
your weeping cousin's gun
as old man tobacco smoke
drifts like a song and
buries the intellectual shadow
beyond stations of memory.

Postmodern Rez Edge Inhalation: Paint Thinner Sublime

Chemical angels ride into this vacant room
as walls and windows drip away
into western fronts, post depression farm
boundaries barely barb-wired together, enclosed
stone pile pastures a gray horse standing still,
facing north, a snort of breath drifting
to a rail car passing horizon
the wind hinting the spirit of ice
nights so long you can only hope
the red blood circling for warmth
in your cells don't freeze here
with the rest of this lost American dream.

How Soon

The story goes from in a rainfall
to sister walking a field
browned autumn. And when she arrives
winter has come, so the old man
rises from his chair, picks up
matches, pipes and tools, and
walks out to begin again.

The sculptures grow by the day,
birds in ice, recognizable
eagles, a bear who began
as a man in a moment of dance.
He does this in ice, all
winter carving at dawn,
carving at dusk.

And sister after walking a field
browned autumn, arrives, watches
from the east window, waits,
goes out to him in spring,
taps him on the shoulder
and points to the pools
of water he's standing over.

Nissway: Directions from the Sovereign of Entelechy

Calendar of Wasted Seasons

Moon of disenrolled families
Moon of bigger per capita
Moon of blackberry teeth
Moon of rotting deer
Moon of knocked over yield sign
Moon of fighting drunken white boys
Moon of mosquito wars
Moon of jet skis
Moon of frightened swans

Gaween—Self Portrait:

I don't believe in self portraits. A person can't live inside a space where face and body are framed static concentrations in contradiction to dynamic eccentricities. A certain bird loves the seed of flowers which bring out the color of the feathers. Yellow flower, black seed, yellow bird, black masks around the flickering eyes, wings tinged by the love for the taste of the seed. Everything is subject to change.

Heads turn to follow blue specks of light floating in corners of a room where gone father called out in sleep, under his own photograph from war places so far away even memory's sun recasts the shadows in those lands.

Hands gather stories, in scars from careless knives, in burns from hot iron and sparks jumping from ashes of pipes, in lines that change as the palms turn over from year to year in story through gesture, from son to old man, to old man moving through dropping leaves in whirls and gusts of wind, talking to the sky, from old man making goods from the hands for other hands to hold.

Words are something else given to change, driven by breath, by hidden charges through secret passages beneath sighted surfaces. Certain words fire recklessly off the tongue jumping through the air without a speaker's volition in a confused chase after hearer. Others are lone votive whispers over colored glassed-in candles. Others are the creation of the hearer, brought forward in tone and rhythm to draw one closer to another and then turned stretched and shaped to create an impossible distance for any one word to travel together with any one word for another. Other words pass unnoticeable. Still others impress themselves on the skin and make skin the bearer of words. Living skin, dead skin, words travel with the skin and continue in long skin processions, in gatherings of words.

I leave words to their own ends. I've seen and heard so many words used with such strange design, I've given up making words take effect. I leave words to their own designs and continue to create with my hands those things which will have the same effects as words. I have remade myself that way, regardless of what the gamblers are doing I have vowed to find Zahquod before the spirit leaves, before the Black River gamblers lose everything. I am creating another portrait here so that I may go back into another older village to find Zahquod.

Letter to the Agency Superintendent:

Dear Mister Master,

Under precisely what conditions

can I get you to tell me the truth?

I ask about your creator

You give me

a book

I ask about your leaders

You give me

a book

I ask about your

people, the old ones

the sick, your women

your children

You give me

a book.

The days go on.

I come to the agency.

You send me away

I have a house full of

books now

It's getting colder

Food is scarce.

I'm looking for ways

to make fire.

November Becomes the Sky
With Suppers for the Dead

I am standing outside
in Minnesota
ghost wind recalling
names in winter mist

The road smells
of dogs two days dead

White photographers talk in
the house of mainstream
media

I can't articulate
the agony of Eagle Singer's
children to them.

We celebrate the old
man while another
generation shoots
crushed and heated
prescriptions
sells baskets,
machinery,
the fixtures yet to be
installed in the house,
yet to be heated
by the tribal government,
for another night
stolen by the stupors
and the wondrous
pleasures of forget
everything medicines.

Back inside
Uncle Two Dogs rolls me
a smoke out of
organic American Spirit

I look to a last cup
of coffee.

The way home
fills with snow
our tracks
human and machine.

Untitled Crow Abstract

Crow echoes drift through
woodfire smoke
names run season to season
silver fish in open palms
startling grouse under chokecherry bush,
autumn fires, steaming insides of deer,
feasts for the dead
ceremonies of passing.

What we haven't forgotten
we haven't lost
What we haven't remembered
we haven't lost
What was before remembrance
remains accessible now
though changed
by what we haven't forgotten
of what we haven't remembered.

Lose yourself in words
the governance of language
scripted identities
backlit shadows of shadows,
turning against wind gusts
crows calling
attracted to animal remains
shadows on winter flat fields
ceremonies of passing.

Windows Against the Rain

We live the same
lies over again

Drawing breath drawing
water drawing rooms
drawing breath

Jamming our hunger
away with white bread
The vegetables of
corporate husbandry
and beasts of set
tables timed as taste
is determined by time

Let us pray this one time
as we breathe
as we eat
one machine to another

from phone call to phone call,
text message to screens
behind screens behind screens

How far we go
through open doors
deepens as our dependency,
becomes more profound.

Letter to the School Superintendent:

Dear Master:

I'm afraid

I cannot return.

I do like school, but

I'm afraid I cannot return.

I have learned

some things,

as you sometimes say,

without question,

but I'm afraid

I cannot return.

I do like school

I have learned,

taken to the meals,

but I'm afraid

I cannot return.

I have learned some things:

to recognize,

for example,

myself in mirrors.

As you sometimes say

it's true,

but I'm afraid

I will not return.

I do like school,

but

the old ones

want me here.

I'm afraid

I will not return.

Yes, the old ones

they are teaching

me Master

to fight the cannibals

and to kill the savage

strangers who keep

coming to us

in lines and colors

through vehicles

and planes

from unknown places.

Primitive Epidermal Song

You see 'em
We have no muses
You see 'em
We give you mooses
You see 'em
We give you lotta tings
We give you lotta tings

We see 'em
You have many muses
We see 'em
You give us your refuses
We see 'em
You take lotta tings
You take lotta tings

We like da houses
But not da homes
We like da brushes
But not the combs
We like da trucks
But not da phones
We like da chicken
But not da bones

You see 'em
We have no paper
You see 'em
We give you words
You see 'em
We give you lotta tings
We give you lotta tings

We see 'em
You have many muses
We see 'em
You give us schoolin'
You take lotta tings
You take lotta tings

We don't like da president
But we like the nickel
We like the hamburger
But not the pickle
We don't like da doctor
But we like the nurse
We don't like the son a bitch
But we learned the curse

You take land
You take words
You make hunting
Your horns and furs
You take children
You take the dead
You make signs
Your names and numbers
You take the spirit
You make water
Your waste and poison
You take the air
You make fire
Your guns and engines

You see 'em
We have no muses
You see 'em
We give, you mooses
You take lotta tings
You take lotta tings

Imperial Lord Woosintoon

Even your best face has two
mouths.
One talks like a social engineer
who keeps his wallet next to his
gun, his bronze trophy wife next to
the telephone, his sons next to the sons
of boys at the anglophilia
boat club, where everyone
wants another shot at a
piece of Cuba.

The other opens for the
endless supply of demands
of pharmaceutical makers,
ingesting while speaking
rhetoric any savior
of the right would never
die for.

My advice to you
take a Cuba Libre
and a day's dosage
of zantac and cappuccino.
Make your own
raft of rubber inner tubes
and no deposit no return plastic,
take your cell phone and
your battery operated
hand held, portable, television,
camera, network connected,
electronic, satellite fed, personal
planner;
better that than to be pushed
from the side of the boat you've

taken out for a party on
the Atlantic coast. Your
ambitious, offspring have been
waiting to set you adrift, waiting
for the moment
when you hit the
water, hoping as they take over
steerage, they can get
away before you drown
and before you realize salvation
was never intended, never the plan
for your own sacrifice.

Abstract on Imperialist Cartographics

There is no map
to liberate you
from the enlargements
of names
the national familiarities
with legends
roads go on
with such transgressions.

You find where you are,
where you'd like to be,
trace the surfaces with
the eye or an index finger.

find a name writ large
go there and remain lost
like all those who in earlier
stages still seek
a code of coordinates.

Song for the One Called Enemy

Remember me when you
sleep among the shifting temper of dream
I will not come for you
Then

Remember me when you
pray for the old man dying in your house
I will not come for you
Then

Remember me as you
eat and drink at the tables of seasonal celebration
I will not come for you
Then

Remember me as you
sing yourself back home from a talk among strangers
I will not come for you
Then

Remember me as you
play with the many faces you believe god or mirrors gave you
I will not come for you
Then

Remember me as you
laugh at some turn of luck in some time of trial
I will not come for you
Then

Remember me as you
dance in circles of circles carried by sound or wind against wind against you
I will not come for you
Then

Remember me as you make
love to some woman you've come to love more than yourself
I will not come for you
Then

Remember me as you
grow tired of grasping for good in every undelivered promise
I will not come for you
Then

Remember me as you
strike out at ghosts in the air, crying into the sky of magnetic distillations, cold and alone
I will find you
Then

Bring you to fire
Then
remind you of all we must have forgotten to be enemies, of all we will carry with us
to release at the end of our days.

Lost Hunter—Under Hidden Constellations

So it is
      winter and the few birds
left at this latitude
wait for you to go face up
whether to dream or death.

You will hear them calling
and calling more as they come
for the eyes first lifting away
from a few moonset frosted limbs.
What is left of stars between
cloud passages
stops the heart between beats
finally catches up to breath
rushing away with skin no
longer yours.

The road beneath your back runs
so long, you know
no way of going, where
fire and story met in
a houseful of names,
where the passages of sun and
shadow over surface and shape
brought you again and again to
the kind of silence you broke
just to say you were not alone.

Another Academic's Last Hope for Coyote Monologue

It's not what you think. It's about respect and what's in your heart. What's in your heart. I know what's in my heart. It's not what you think. I offered tobacco, got permission from four elders, two were direct descendents of coyote, one of them, an old clan mother, made lunch for me. We talked for a long time, almost two hours. I told her "I got a good heart." "Go ahead," she said "It's what's in your heart. Bring him back by Monday," she said.

It's not what you think. It's about respect. I cited his tribe. Talked about his place in your stories. I prayed over it. When I spoke about him, he was right there with me. I swear. He didn't object. He didn't say *that's not how the story goes*. He didn't stop me from making his story the subject of my lecture. He was right there with me. He stood up there with me. It's not what you think. People loved the lecture. They understood the talk, the stories. They laughed at the story of his lost balls. Old white scholars shook my hand. Women came to us. Sure he got away from me a few times. He's coyote. Besides I always found him. Sure we slept with a few people. He's coyote. Who am I to deny him. Women came to us. People loved the lecture. Yes, we got drunk after the keynote. How was I to know he couldn't handle California Shiraz. He's coyote and it felt good being there with him, talking about him. I know he seems different now. We'll take him to a dentist, replace those missing teeth. He's not the same coyote, but it's not what you think. Anyway, I brought him back, just like I promised. My heart is good that way. I keep my promises. I know he's not the same. I know he smells different. I know he seems fluffier, softer, a bit more pensive, but maybe if we leave him alone for awhile, maybe if he sticks around for awhile, he'll be the old coyote again. Maybe he'll go out and get down in the dirt again. Maybe he'll forget what happened, or maybe you can talk with him. Maybe he'll get his voice back. Put him up on the hill. Maybe he'll get his voice back. He's coyote. I'm sure he'll get his voice back. I know in my heart he'll get his voice back. He's coyote.

Simple Four Part Directions for Making Indian Lit

Ah-Beshig for the money:
Take something Indin
and take something
non
Indin
Make the Indin
indigenous or native
or skin

Make the
non
Indin
non
indigenous or
non
native
or non
skin
or white

Ah-Two: for the shonyaa
make the Indin non Indin
and the non Indin Indin
or the white Indin

Ah-T(h)ree:
Make a character out of paper
write a name with fire
or sky, or a combination of
color and the names of birds
or the absence of an article
with a present tense verb
from a limited number of infinitives
(you may) include prepositions,

except: forego, between, beyond, under
over, into, across, beside, beneath;
avoid abstractions, slang, economic terms,
hip phrases, or contemporary
situations or signs.

(You cannot use, for example, the names

>   *Foregoes Hawk*
>   *Under Crow*
>   *Into Deer*
>   *Values Dog*
>   *or Love Crane*
>   *or Dances Similar*
>   *or In the Middle of Night*
>   *Red Thunder Banging*
>   *or*
>   *Across Wolf*
>   *Eating Horse*
>   *Bling Eagle*
>   *or Has in Trust*
>   *or Many Shoes*
>   *or Sun Dude*
>   *or Chick Lit*
>   *or Donut Shop*
>   *Yard Sale Man*
>   *Beneath the Ground*
>   *Upside the Head*
>   *Do not Cross*
>   *or Out of Position*
>   *or Big Credit*
>   *or Bear Pimp*

or Stone Suitcase
or Ice Cream Turtle
or Calls the Taxi
or Waits for Bus
or Bums a Smoke
or Speaks the Bible
Running Mascara
or Saint Muskrat
or Grafitti Clouds
or Air Flute
or Telescope Woman
or Medicine Cheese
or Karma Bull
or Missus Layups
or Nice One
or Red Exit
or Off Limits
Or even
Working Man)

So, maybe take a break
offer prayers to the polytheistic
Indo European Spirits
of syntax.

Inscribe a smoke or a ceremony

Add laughter to fighting
tears to anything
sounding like history;
reinscribe Indian
Non Indian
White.

Repeat Smoke Smudge Rinse Repeat

Imperialism
    conquest
Imperialism disease medicine
    conquest alcohol
Imperialism guns bow
    conquest
Imperialism

Make language of crossing tongues
as simple as pow wow for profit
and dying chevy hey yaw
as complex as Aristotle remains ethical
and remains remain catalogued.
Use newspapers, magazines, museum brochures,
skatagon, flint and match;
roll characters, names, words, onto paper
paper into rolls
rub with bear grease and lard,
or last night's ground beef leavings
(this will not work with
olive or sunflower oil.)
Say four hail marys, a couple of
Aho's or ah ah kaweekin
Ignite all of the above

Ah-Forza:
After all this becomes lit.
Be careful about who you
read to:

They may be hearing
Indin in everything
non Indin

(As what remains from fire is not spirit)

Hope Returns a Lost Whistle

We call Hope
Two Bears, knowing
Hope is bi-polar
(not to denigrate bears or people
who suffer mood swings
since her brother Two Dogs
claims everyone is a little bi-polar.)

But let me say this, when my
whistle turned up missing
from the poplar shaker
on my stall
at the thirsty dance
Hope had it. How she got it
no one knows.

Enter the clown spirit
I try to give him the
Black pipe, but he and his
clown wife prefer
chasing children with
a pine branch broom and
aiming a bow and arrow
too small to shoot at
offerings on the ground.

It was too hot to do
anything but laugh
I was too thirsty to
see humor unless
humor came looking
for me.

Eventually even a
clown likes a smoke
So he took the pipe
down
upside
smoking like a clown

Then the world stood right again,
the oldest Little Boy sang,
the dancers danced fasting,
and everyone, in the
circle, in the making
of some distant dream,
including Hope,
went back to
prayer, calling with
every breath
through hollow bones.

If Only John Ashberry Were Gregory Corso, If Only Gregory Corso Was the Terra Cotta Horse on the Coffee Table With a Magazine Open to the You Can Be An Artist Ad.

Morning's another mouthful of smoke, somewhere in this land of little vegetable labels, another dog is chained to a northern laundry pole with no lines running between it and its rusting southern double, casting a T shadow.

Two Vowels, the Anishinabe linguist of no standardized federal extract, has left another series of ethical questions on my answering machine, which I will not respond to until I know he will not pick up his own phone, as he will be sleeping in a skin of bear grease under a blanket of flying horses, with a woman whose intelligence remains more powerful in silence than in all of his spoken words.

Must the questions always be released under the same ritual of the pointing finger pulling away from the button reading messages:

If someone gives me tobacco to give to someone else for a name do they have to give me gas money to get the offering to the namer?

Do we have to use the same species of trees for the ceremony this year?

Can I sweat with the women of a tribe who will tell sacred stories to strangers even when there's no snow on the ground?

What color cloth should I bring to the feast for the last thunder at the urban traditional's house?

How many pipes should I smoke to make the sun dry the tears on my father's grave?

Did you hear the one about the tribal planner and the Republican lobbyist?

Is it okay to harvest strawberries in view of the cemetery?

After I burn wood what's the proper prayer for remembering the wood as I smell the smoke on my jacket in the frozen food section of the Red Owl store?

I hit a turkey on the freeway, should I eat it or offer it to the soup kitchen people?

Did you ever find that gambling medicine your Aunt used the night she won on the dolphin slot machines?

Do I have to smudge my corolla after every oil change or do I have to have an oil change if I smudge my corolla every three thousand miles?

What kind of Indian would Jesus be, if Jesus was Indian?

Is that gambling medicine green and do little clusters of buds stick to your hands when you go to harvest it?

Can my wife wear my grandmother's golden cross to the next ghost supper?

What time should I come for the singing?

Can I bring my cousin the sniper contractor who just got back from Kandahar?

After awhile all machines are like answering machines, they fill up and there's no room for anything human inside. So I pass the housed image of my glassed transparent ghost self with the wind antics of exterior branches. I go where I always go after one machine is full. I get a cup of coffee and empty another. Then I pick up the phone and touch the numbers, the letters, the signs, all points of transmission. A lost voice hides in a sonic code vibration, in a persistent resonant hiss, waiting to crack open the night, splitting vowels, breaking infinitives of infinitives,

to go line by line, from a room with a terra cotta horse, a sleeping dog, an ashtray of many camel butts, a magazine open to a "you can be an artist too" ad

to a room Two Vowels may never go into again, a hallway away oh hey from the dream consonant anarchy of his stuttering apnia: after all

to hear what I have said, instead of what I am saying, he will not be in the same sunstruck morning space of more questions for his rapidly filling answering machine.

Directions to the Sovereign of Entelechy

    After two rings

I hear you
a voice negotiating static
modulations
hisses and whispers of
futures and the latest losses
not of land, not of time, not of memory.

I imagine you
between lights
bardo emotions, a few
violet phosphenes under streetlamps,
speaking into a cell phone
before the school ruins,
before writing on
eroded graffito walls with
the name of every Indian
who ever worked among whites

    Chief

(Beneath that
Another name)

    Angel

Nothing changes,
walls tell what
can't be told
in schools

Loves

Lost between us

Through the interference
you asking me
the best way
to get back home.

Neewin: After Zahquod

Calendar of Wasted Seasons

Moon of woman forgetting heartbreak
Moon of missing relatives
Moon of Blue Thunder Boy Feast
Moon of too many baskets
Moon of missing prescriptions
Moon of glazed trees
Moon of the lost watch
Moon of the faraway burial

Ahwosso—Past

I am alone and poor, seeking a dream to carry me, a hawk wind, or a bird with a human voice, clear, resolute, with instructions, or an act of some kind, a motion in trees, a moving star, a band of light on a stone face, or a painted old man, or woman, or child, walking toward me, human to bear to human. These things may not come, but I wait, alone and poor, where I choose to blacken my face with sweat fire ashes, seeking space where undergrowth shadow blossoms into, ridge hill, morning light, where I find an ascendable arboreal ancestor, as invisibly earth rooted as visibly sky branched, less like a family than an explosion of dark heavy aspirations, checked by wind crossing, the weight of birds, the seed end of flowers, the brittle end of leaves.

> Who will you become
>
> will you become
>
> What name
>
> will you carry
>
> What song
>
> will you bring back
>
> Who will you become

I am tired of dreaming, tired of the hot wind, the cold wind, who takes away my face with each breath.

The animal came first, out of the mist, separating from vaporous dawn, running, full of life, then struck suddenly inert, it fell, legs buckling, the body turning, even as it met earth, on an incline and gave up in gasps, through the smoking wound in the flank, through air from black nostrils.

The old man walked up later, to the crest of the incline where the animal had fallen. When he came to the deer, he spoke, words, I could not hear from where I sat in the tree. Then the old man made his way around to the animal head, he kneeled and looked into the eyes. He went on talking as he set down his rifle and took a pack from his back. He pulled out tobacco, held it to the sky and he sprinkled the offering on the ground, in front of the eyes of the dead animal. He stood then and dropped more tobacco along the body, over the head. He covered the head with black cloth, went silent for a moment and he began singing. This much I could hear, though parts were whispers and parts were drawn into thin wind breaths with the calls of crows and whistling of jays.

>Waaskesh
>
>it has been
>
>a good life
>
>Waashkesh
>
>i give thanks
>
>for your life.
>
>Waaskesh
>
>for all the days

> you have lived
>
> Waashkesh
>
> i give thanks
>
> Waashkesh
>
> for the good life
>
> you have lived
>
> i give thanks

Then the old man drew a knife blade across the deer's throat and let blood and he began to cut deep into the deer. The old man severed glands, pulled out intestines, took away from the steaming insides of the animal, precisely and carefully. Some of what he took he placed on the ground beside him, parts of the animal he would leave behind, for other animals, who would come later.

When the old man cut away the heart he stood up. The heart was a shining dead violet, almost black, a whisper of steam in his hands. The old man spoke again, his words rolled over the glistening face of the heart in cool fog disappations of his breath. He reached into his bag, gathered more material, spread the red cloth out on the ground. He rolled the heart into the material with the tobacco and tied them together with strips of blue cloth.

After that, he walked to a place where a big gray stone rose out of the earth. The old man took the heart over there: he talked to the sky, he held the heart to the sun, he turned in many directions; he looked down to the earth under his feet. When he quit talking the old man set the heart on the stone. He placed some more tobacco there in a circle around the heart. He circled the stone with tobacco.

Then the old man was gone, a trudging backlit memory, dragging the dead animal behind him.

I had been in the tree for a long time. I had had no vision. Yes, the days were more gradual than the days back at home, but the fast had become full of ordinary sound and sense, of sun crossings, shadow extensions and animal movements. I had grown tired of watching and soon I went to sleep.

My dreams took me out of myself again. I found myself looking into faces around a fire. There were old people speaking, casting blue sparks into glowing rings of words. I was looking back at the earth, at villages in autumn, at the people moving across the earth in families. I drew closer to people, I became one of them, a child with a face blackened with ashes, walking into the village after having been gone for a long, long time.

Loud echoes woke me. In full sun crows floated overhead, drifting like black paper ashes, communicating shadow crossings with other crows in tree branches. A crow came out of the sky then and landed on the gray stone where the heart lay. The crow nudged the heart and began pecking at the cloth. I came down from the tree and ran to the stone, calling back to the crows. "Go," I yelled, "get away, go, go, go." I made a song out of "go" and go echoes of go and I ran in circles around the stone as I sang, waving my arms and jumping.

Maybe I was wrong then. Maybe I should have stayed in the tree. But I sang the crows away and the heart remained on the stone.

And I didn't go back to the tree. Maybe that was wrong. Instead, I remained there, circling the stone, watching, protecting the old man's offering, keeping the animals away from the heart.

When I tired of walking, of circling, I slept on the ground next to the stone. I don't know how many days passed, suns came and went and no one came for me. In time, air cooled, leaves drifted in the woods around the clearing there. No one came for me. Sun to sun, I just kept circling the heart on the stone.

Song for a Sister
Who Won't Let Go

When Zahqoud died
you could not say
Baa maa api

You could not even
raise your eyes to greet
even the most distant
of relatives or the
closest of visitors.

You left silence between
yourself and the northern oriole
singing over sections
of orange on the rail
beneath the thermometer
face.

You turned instead
from memory to memory
to find memory always
behind or awaiting another
present of some sensual
association, like a luminous
guide hollowing a place
for us out of this good
Earth.

Guessing at the Weight of Spirit

You sink into glass
The moon a gift sifted
through the vitreous
turned over by lens

by transfigurations
the mind drawn
old roads
ghost houses
suppers in winters
of cold cracking
trees

the ones sitting
across from you
stare vacantly
speaking only names
whispered beyond whorls
of reworked

tobacco shadows
a thousand ways
of seeing this and still
none as in this dreaming
as if dead.

Profile of a Black River Member

(A Thinner Narrative)

State cops took
a second set of keys
to his suv
for the second time.

He got out of some seven
codes of conduct red way
rehabilitation center

Got his stomach stapled
with a June per capita check

Lost sixty pounds

Left his wife and two
boys under five on a blanket
at the tribal fireworks

Took up with local
city councilwoman
who brought him home
to a bedroom full of mirrors

In November you saw him
at a Ghost Supper,
eating only berries.

He told you
he was always looking for
something better

Remembering Shadow:
In the Art of Not Crying
For Ray

So your woman's
a Mormon angel
who gave you a
boy named Shadow

Your comedic voices
like dark bars better
than your housefire
skin likes Eagleheart
sweats

But the clown pose
goes once you
succumb to the
sadness of medication
and your four-day-old
son in a casket

Gay goo maa wee kay
Gay goo mish shii shay

Remember the passing
train a twisting Doppler
Crescendo lip sync
in the sermon of some
Latter Day saint speak

Remember the early
white moon above
the redtail turn

Gaygoo naa waa paa me koo nah
binishay

as we sang from
the thirsty dance cycle
and watched your
boy Shadow go
into the ground.

Rez Edged Suicide Muse

The less dramatic seek a life of wine, or some deeper down downer, brainkiller inhalants for the poorer, paint thinner, some non-stick aerosol maybe; some go deeper into winter until January snow makes the road away from home impassable, return better than the too drawn out hope of freezing; some seek the solace of spectators, watching the same games over and over, as some follow insomnia on streets plowed toward cold lurid dawn.

In this place pain doesn't speak, it inhabits, it tithes remorse, slits skin quick exits, ties ropes to rafters, then backs down the ladder, refuses to answer phones, lets letters fill the mailbox, feeds the moods of oligarch shadows; there are more ways of doing this than all the recounts of all dark nights; so, hang fifty year old larger than memory photographs on walls intended to keep others out. Talk all you want, she won't say: *conversation only goes so far, dies in the hum of machinery, in the creak of a house of nothing else to do but sleep.*

It would be useless to try to hear what suicide says anyway. She has her own sub tonal music, cast in a theatre of lip sync, in dispersions of frost, in lines at a cemetery service, where wind stirs into grit into faces, despair blows holes open in the earth; she imagines song, your own voice, godspeak coming out of the ground, saying something, saying you'll always be welcome here in the earth.

Oshawanung Manido Equay

This wing feather
I give you

Not for love
Not for memory
Not for the hidden bone
Beneath the smooth blue down
Not for the shadow it
Brushes away in your hand
Not in exchange for promises
Whispered over the gold moon
At you ear
Not for the mist that rolls
From your lips to cross
The morning sunflowers
In gray air
Not for the man I
Want you to forget
Not for a moment
Not for moving smoke
Or hot days
Not for the lies I gave
For the stories I told
Not for the dreamtime
Artist who keeps you awake
At night
Not for the power
To hold off collection agents
Not to remove layers of dust
From possession of the dead
Or distant
Not to put out the candle
You've lit in prayer
Not to gather your amazement

And release it as my own
Not for you to excite my skin
Not for fletching
For any kind of arrow
Not for floating free
For a few moments above
Ground in an August whirlwind
Not to represent the stone
I found it on
Not that you may fly
Or walk differently
Not so the wing will come
Back as a whole bird
For me when I am starving
Or alone

No, this wing feather I give
You who know
I can't fly
You who know
I will.

White Cloud Woman through a Southern Window

After all these funeral autumns, of diminishing light, revealing syllabary forms of maple, ash, ironwood and beech, children still gather around, under a growing collection of statuary, the youngest for comfort in tears, the oldest waiting for dinner, cash, keys to the explorer.

Meanwhile outside the window where the reckless redtail snapped his neck, whether toward clarity or reflection, beyond the living room depth, with the birdcall clock singing at eight, the voice of an electronic warbler

Your garden has taken on another life, the stone angel in the center of the fountain has weathered some, seems even to be blending into the designs and umbrage of tree.

Sonny's Wake 2000

After Joe Mitigoons prays
with the bear pwaagun
After Waabizii and the boys
from Pine Point make
the vocal ascension
to sing some honor song

Wandering children hear
this school's janitor ghost
in the hallways
during the Catholic liturgy.

We all pass
the floral presentations
the messages of regret
the army decorations
a golden gloves fight card
the arrangements of photos
the last of a thinner man
his foot on the front bumper
of a red galaxy

Ahead of us a few
of the old ones—
Leech Lake hymn
singers—genuflect,
then kneel.
Steady eyed before
the silver casket
they whisper so
softly the movement
of our skin
in our best clothes
is all we hear.

White Cloud Woman at Dawn

After Zahquod disappeared
into the village of pines
where you were both raised
under a sky
flowing with your name
toward a distance of HUD home roofs
a couple with wooden aerials.

The singers I was told
returned to uncle's place
where he foamed at the mouth
in a heartstopping overdose
of crack a few urban dealers
had cooked in the basement
with the blown out wall
opposite the hanging regalia
of Bright Sky the grandfather
who died dancing on the west coast.
This was also where Uncle
kept the raccoon who'd wandered
up out the rushes years before
Irene crossed over and before his 3rd
wife Dream Babe hooked up with
some young felon over a September
barrel fire at a party near
Little Earth projects.

Whether residents of star road myth
or Catholic cemetery earth
you don't mention
the names much anymore

This is just part of
morning prayer, thanks
outlasting so much memory
going out daily with tobacco
being surrounded
by unidentified light
looking back at the deer
people staring back at you
then watching them all
turning to run,
at the sound
of a door closing somewhere
turning over jumping
fallen beech, knifing
back through gauze wrapped
cedar, back toward the river
beyond your view
in the last whispered
tracks of your breath.

Dodem Dream Song

Old Man
I will guide your silver canoe
to the center of the water
where the loon father carries
children on his back.

If I am quiet
I will arrive as a call
from another shore
to draw close enough
to see the fantastic eyes
seeing me drifting
alone.

Recount to a Black River Elder

Before the end

I was troubled by the antelope carvings
of your brother and by the time your
partner waited seemingly
lost in the dark with your name
while you waded through a field of snow
from the overturned automobile
that held the center for all your
journeys of lies.

This may seem grim,
but do not be troubled by
lost art.

When the talking earth people come home
for the Black River funeral feast, will there be
anyone there to tell their prototype
intellectuals
X minus signature = treaty?
Who will ask these geniuses
Y sovereignty is less than null
and the numerator of next to
the other side of
nothing over a denominator
of what it costs
to feed a village of cowboy oligarchs,
even as they grease the roads and oil only
the Indins, of great revenues—you know,
the ones with big pixel coming attractions
of ends to means to ends of
hospitality?

Whatever that once was
is under the management of new constructions
of tribal identity.

>   If you can inscribe it
>   It is said
>   It is not saying
>   What it is.

All this may seem grim, but do not
be troubled by lost gains.

This is where I imagine you'll go
from here.
(It won't be across the very silver river
or on some black road, or into some luminous
tunnel where you'll pass through
shadow after shadow to find
Wahsaygeeshig and all others
of numberless names in brightness;
It won't have anything to do with
alien craft, a white canoe with no paddles
gliding of some unknown accord, or with
you flying off like a parade balloon
while seeing yourself below
set for long sleep in a silver box.)

Yes, you will enter the skin of another
through the eyes, (the reverse
retinal image of the light you
stood in after your father's
last surgery on a second organ)
July wind on the face, with the image

of Here and There Woman
above pledge cloths,
where you stand downwind from cedar
a final grasp of the finger
of the same Little Star who pointed
to Smoke's dancing horse.

You will move with the skin of another
You will stand with them when they
stand, you will walk with them when
they walk. You will tell them
so many things
under the sun, like how much not to
believe and how many tons of feathers
it takes to make a story of a powwow
smell like a circle of thirsty dance cedar
smudge on flesh offering sunday and
feel like a hand over
Yellowhammer beadwork

You will tell them and you will
continue telling until you jump
into the silver water yourself,
or take the mystery canoe
toward the polestar
or set out on the road

You will tell them stories.
They will in turn tell stories
there is no end in telling.

Pipestone: The Best Conversations That Never Took Place

Between the mouth of a cave and a tobacco colored waterfall

We stand on a bridge

At the quarry a blue heron ascends from a shallow creek, gray wings

Open against red stone strata

I want to tell you of faces there
a way of imagining earth
imagining us Zahquod, Eagleheart
and Wahsay Geeshig

But, we walk instead to higher ground
to wider views, fields of blown
grass, roads beyond roads,
some horizon of shifting western fronts

Then, we return to vehicles, travel and go
on forgetting beneath
a moon separating from cloud

Before the Thirsty Dance

Crossing Sky claimed clowns
hold the poles of this world
between magnetic
north and south we find balance

I reach across the table hand him an
American Spirit

What you see here he says that is not it
What you see here is not it

That August his mother died
He wore the same armless
sweatshirt for two weeks
a piece of masking tape
across the chest
read in blue ink
I love you Mom

Once inside the car
outside the white church
he told me
"I know who killed her"

Somehow all dreaming leads
to this: our clowns tire;
their grip loosens
we feel the vibration
with each foot we plant
in misery and
laughter clowns make

A Black River Elder Pretends

to be a haiku master
while speaking to a petrified
box turtle

The volume of a
pond resounds with
a glazed history of
long winter sleeping

Between yellow water
lilies you return with
the fingerprints of a child
on your back

On your entry into water
fish come to stillness beneath
you as you carry a few moments
on land in your hot blood

You will never again
escape from water or sun.

Even with the rest of you
inside, your tail remains
attached outside, a
reminder to those
who would speak to you

you are still there
but must remain hiding.

Traveling Among Strangers

This song is not from our language. These sounds came out of the dark where I was traveling among strangers in sadness. This song made a circle of light around me where I was traveling in sadness among strangers. These sounds made a circle of light in the darkness. This song is not from our language. These sounds came from a singer sitting across from me in a circle of light. This song made light where I was traveling in darkness. These sounds took away the sadness I was traveling in. This song is not in any language. These sounds came from a singer in a circle of light. This song took away my sadness. This song is not in any language. When I awake I will sing this song. My father is traveling in sadness among strangers in the dark. When I awake I will sing this song. This song will take away the sadness of my dead father.

Zahquod's Land

Tell the boy who makes memories
Those ghosts have gone home hungry again

The offspring of eloquent leaders of broken clan lines
are face up in the mission cemeteries where the only
prayers pass in funeral time and board fires take down homes
one plank at a time

There is nothing
no one will offer here
Even thunder gets no tobacco
New names receive no smoke,
No material
Just as there are no gifts for harvest
No acknowledgement upon reception
of water or entry onto lakes and rivers
and no one makes fires to sanction
meetings or talk anymore

Only remembrance relocates a missing wall
A surface lost under partial moon to night
dogs calling
Unknown movements wary
Unknown movements hearing
the way we infer sounds of strangers,
walking in places on earth where everyone
is supposed to be accounted for

It isn't that we must give something for time
or that we must pay for use of space
What we make of the gift of memory like
what we've lost in habits hides in what
will be found in returns of what seems
beyond substance

Iron nails in black ash
block foundations overgrown
ceramic fragments from plates
held out full to travelers long ago
in rooms, where the old ones told us,
where all the speakers inhabiting this place
reminded us, we always had a home
among them.

Blue Thunder Boy Healing Song
For Ray

        Bodies and faces
Severed by shadow
            Made whole by sun light
                    Come out of those dark rooms

Turn from the constant blue radiance
        of those high definition
        screens of people who only want to keep
        you still
        until you too are confined
        to a chair, a spoon fed spectator

We are waiting for you
where
Wind turns fire smoke
where
Stones take in heat
where
A white cedar tail waits
in a container of water

We will sing
in the dark there
where our voices seem
one voice from so
many directions
of so many people
without measure
of distance or time.

www.ingramcontent.com/pod-product-compliance
Lightning Source LLC
Chambersburg PA
CBHW031136090426
42738CB00008B/1112